Original title:
Life, Laughter, and Missing Socks

Copyright © 2025 Creative Arts Management OÜ
All rights reserved.

Author: Theodore Sinclair
ISBN HARDBACK: 978-1-80566-159-7
ISBN PAPERBACK: 978-1-80566-454-3

A Symphony of Stray Socks

In the dryer's warm embrace,
Odd pairs dance in playful grace.
Cotton blues and polka dots,
Each one lost, yet each one's caught.

A red sock winks at a green,
Laughing at their quirky scene.
Missing mates, a grand debut,
Together, they'll still make a crew.

Solemn Socks and Joyful Antics

Once paired neatly in a drawer,
Now they play on the laundry floor.
Stripes and spots, they twist and shout,
The missing ones just stomp about.

A solemn sock with faded lines,
Joins in with giggles, playful signs.
They scatter forth like embers bright,
In silly games, they find their light.

The Enigma of the Laundry Monster

Whispers of a sneaky beast,
Who dines on socks from west to east.
Missing mates, the tales they share,
A laundry monster, caught unaware.

Beneath the spin, the chaos hums,
Where mismatched mayhem surely comes.
It gobbles threads and whispers glee,
Creating puzzles, wild and free.

Yarn Dreams and Laundry Nightmares

As night falls on the spinning fluff,
The yarn begins to weave its stuff.
In shadows dance the threads of fate,
Unraveled dreams, they celebrate.

A tangle here, a knot formed there,
With sock puppets in the air.
They tell their tales, so bold and bright,
In laundry's realm, they own the night.

Whispers of Forgotten Footwear

In corners where shadows play,
Old companions fade away.
They danced and jogged without a care,
Now solo, they silently stare.

A left, a right, a twist of fate,
Together they once were first-rate.
Now lonely in their cozy nook,
Their stories lost, like a good book.

The Mystery of Disappearing Pairs

A sock slips through the dryer's grin,
Where does it go, oh where've you been?
Invisible portals in washing spins,
Creating chaos with cheeky grins.

Each time I find a single mate,
I ponder fate and calculate.
Where once were two, now only one,
A riddle wrapped in fabric fun.

Giggles in the Laundry Room

The washer hums a lively tune,
As socks conspire beneath the moon.
A playful game of hide and seek,
Their laughter bubbles, soft and cheeky.

Caught in a tumble, they let loose,
Whirling like dancers, what a ruse!
The scent of fresh in every fold,
Adventures spun, and tales retold.

Unmatched Tales of Soles

A tale of woe for a lonely heel,
Riding solo, it learns to feel.
Its partner lost in the wash of time,
A solitary sock, with rhythm and rhyme.

Yet in every mismatch, stories swell,
Of journeys taken, oh can't you tell?
For in a drawer, secrets lie,
Waiting for laughter to amplify.

The Whimsy Beneath the Bed

Underneath the bed they play,
A sock parade goes on today.
Mismatched colors, stripes a-flare,
Join the dance with carefree flair.

Dust bunnies cheer, they've found a friend,
In a cotton world that knows no end.
With laughter echoing in the night,
These little socks bring pure delight.

Sock Puppets and Shenanigans

Two bright socks with goofy eyes,
Stage a show amidst the sighs.
They wiggle, smile, put on a show,
While humans watch and never know.

The voices squeak in silly tone,
As old cans rattle, all alone.
In this realm of fabric fun,
The sock puppets outshine the sun.

Tattered Reminders of Joy

Faded patterns, stories untold,
Each little tear, a moment bold.
They whisper secrets of playful fights,
And joyful mischief in lost delights.

Worn-out threads from endless spins,
Frame the laughter, where joy begins.
A drawer full of memories so sweet,
Tattered tokens of happy feet.

Giggles in the Stitches

Stitches hold tales of festive cheer,
While mismatched pairs draw us near.
With a giggle here and a chuckle there,
They spin a yarn, a woolly affair.

With every step, a giggle grows,
As wandering socks plot their shows.
In the chaos of a laundry spree,
These silly socks just want to be free.

Chasing Giggles in the Breeze

A butterfly flutters near my nose,
Chasing after it, off balance, I doze.
The sun pokes fun with a golden ray,
As I stumble, laughing my cares away.

A squirrel darts by with acorn in tow,
We share a glance, then I burst out in flow.
The trees are chuckling, swaying in glee,
As I trip and tumble, so wild and free.

Socks That Wandered Too Far

A sock slips away on a wild summer day,
Wandering off, it now thinks it can play.
It dances on grass, makes friends with the bees,
While I search high and low among all the trees.

The other sock pouts, feeling left in the drawer,
"Hey, what's up with that? I thought we had more!"
But one sock is off, living life like a star,
While I keep on searching, dreaming bizarre.

Echoes of Joy in the Laundry Room

In the spin cycle, the shirts start to sway,
While socks tell stories of their wild escapade.
A whiff of fresh fabric, a soft tumble's delight,
Whispers and giggles float deep in the night.

The dryer sings softly, a tune of its own,
As the clothes go round, the laughter's full grown.
Each fold and crease has a tale to unfold,
In the warm, cozy chaos, adventures retold.

The Great Sock Escape

Two socks conspired, little rebels at heart,
While I turned my back, they plotted their start.
With a jump and a whirl, they jumped from the pile,
Braving the world with a cheeky sock smile.

Adventures await, under beds and beneath,
Conquering dust bunnies, hiding their sheath.
They giggle and run, little fugitives bold,
While I shake my head, their antics unfold.

Tales from the Bottom of the Basket

In the depths of laundry's domain,
Odd pairs roam like wild terrain.
A striped fellow seeks his mate,
While polka dots contemplate fate.

Whispers of cotton tell tall tales,
Of clandestine trips, of windy gales.
Beneath the dryer, they plot and scheme,
In search of a world that's not just a dream.

Each fold and wrinkle, a silent cheer,
For socks that spin without a peer.
These textile rebels laugh and play,
In a carnival dance, they sway away.

Amidst the chaos, a sock parade,
Where mismatched footies aren't afraid.
From basket depths, their stories spring,
A vibrant chorus of fabric sings.

Joyful Chaos of Textile Adventures

Beneath the bed, a sock mob forms,
In colorful patterns, breaking norms.
They tumble out with giggles galore,
Daring the dust bunnies to settle the score.

With polka dots prancing and stripes that twirl,
They hold a party, a fabric whirl.
Daring adventures in the laundry land,
Where fibers unite, an unplanned band.

A mismatched crew, yet spirits high,
They leap and bound, they touch the sky.
In echoes of fun, they pave their way,
Through socks and tales that warmly play.

When washers spin, their laughter rings,
As detergent fades, joy still clings.
In this wild dance, beats never cease,
A playful journey, a sock's blissful peace.

Renegade Fabrics and Silly Smiles

In a land where fabrics go rogue,
Cheeky patterns burst from the fold.
They giggle as they slip and slide,
Escaping confines, nowhere to hide.

A frayed hem whispers secrets bright,
As mismatched hues twirl in delight.
With every step, a silly grin,
They leap from their basket, let chaos begin.

Squishy and squirmy, they revel in glee,
As socks unite in a soft jubilee.
Their secret mission? To spread pure cheer,
In halls of laundry, they vanish sheer.

They squeak and squeal with every spin,
A dance of fabric, where all win.
With colors shouting, they laugh and sway,
In their joyous world, they forever play.

The Sock's Somersault

A daring sock took a leap one day,
In a twist of fate, it rolled away.
With a flip and a flutter, it spun in delight,
Chasing the dryer, oh what a sight!

It somersaulted past the lint trap's hold,
With threads of adventure, bright and bold.
In its journey, it met a furry mate,
Together they danced, weaving fate.

Through hallways they pranced, a merry chase,
In the wild sandbox, they found their place.
Tickled by feet and sunny beams,
They laughed and leaped in cotton dreams.

At dusk, they returned, a pair once more,
With stories woven in their fabric lore.
A sock's escapade, a whimsical tale,
Of playful spins in a world so frail.

Socks that Sing in the Wash

In the spin of the cycle, they dance with delight,
Colors collide in a whirl of sheer flight.
One sock is a crooner, the other a clown,
Together they tumble, the stars of the town.

When the door swings open, they tumble and hop,
Hiding their secrets where nobody's stopped.
Each wink from the dryer, a giggle, a tease,
They'll joke about missing—oh, if you please!

So gather your pair, give a shout to the crew,
In the land of the laundry, they sing just for you.
Though one may go rogue, on a caper unseen,
The duet continues, with joy unforeseen.

So chuckle and cheer, for the socks in the wash,
They'll brighten your day, like a colorful posh.
When they come out to play, you'll laugh till you drop,
With socks that are singing, the fun never stops.

Tangles of Joy in the Fabric of Days

Amid every stitch lies a tale to be spun,
A misfit in fabric, a race never run.
Snagged in the closet, they plot and conspire,
With twirls and with twists, to lift hearts higher.

A contention of colors, a tussle of thread,
Each longing for freedom, for adventures ahead.
With humor contagious, they frolic and jive,
Braiding the moments where laughter's alive.

In pockets of pockets, they hide and they seek,
Whispering secrets at the dusk of the week.
Each fold holds a belly laugh, pure and sweet,
As joy's tangled up where new memories meet.

So cherish those pieces, the mix and the match,
With every pairing, enchantment we'll catch.
To sip from the mug of the silly and fun,
In the fabric of days, the laughter's begun.

A Playful Journey Through Peculiar Footwear

Two feet in a frenzy, they're off on a spree,
With mismatched companions, just wait and see!
The left is all polka, the right has a stripe,
In a world of the quirky, they're the ones ripe.

From puddles to parks, they stomp every beat,
With giggles adorning, they skip down the street.
In every step taken, there's mischief in tow,
Each clumsy adventure, a new way to glow.

They gallop through sunbeams, they dodge every shoe,
In a misfit parade, they'll coax out a view.
The strangeness combined makes the dull moments bright,

With every small shuffle, they dance into light.

So march in your journey, embrace the bizarre,
With a sprinkle of weirdness, you'll go very far.
Yes, footwear's a canvas where laughter's displayed,
With playful adventures that never will fade.

Laughter Stitched in Every Seam

Through every seam stitched, a chuckle awaits,
A fluffy good morning, as sunshine creates.
When buttons bring banter and zippers delight,
The fun starts unfolding from day into night.

With pockets of giggles, and cuffs lined with cheer,
They'll tease and they'll tickle, no worries, just clear.
In the weave of existence, those threads will combine,
Creating a tapestry that's simply divine.

So don your odd garments, together they'll shine,
With the patchwork of joy, feeling simply sublime.
The mirror reflects you, a whimsical guise,
Each outfit a story, with laughter that flies.

So cherish each fiber, each knot, and each turn,
For the joy in the seams, we all get to learn.
With a hop and a skip, we'll embrace all we see,
In this festive ensemble, let humor run free!

The Silhouette of a Lonely Sock

In the drawer, it sits alone,
A mismatched dream, a tale of its own.
Its partner vanished in the night,
Leaving it here to ponder its plight.

With every tumble, it yearns to roam,
A journey seek for a place called home.
It twirls in rhythm, a dance so bold,
In a world where pairs are bought and sold.

Yet here it waits, in patient despair,
With a smile stitched on like it doesn't care.
Every glance at the floor, a mischievous glance,
That maybe, just maybe, it'll find a chance.

Oh, the one who walks with a single shoe,
Never knows the antics a sock can do.
A circus performer, that's what it dreams,
In a theater of laundry, where laughter beams.

Whirling Threads in the Air

In the spinning world of rumbling sheets,
A ballet unfolds with tiny feats.
Colors collide in a vibrant swirl,
As handpicked favorites begin to twirl.

One blue sock tangoes with polka dots,
An ensemble cast, no tangled knots.
They leap and spin, full of flair,
Laughing in joy, a dance in the air.

Yet, in this charade, one sock turns shy,
Hiding away, letting the bold ones fly.
But fear not, dear friend, take a brave stance,
Join in the fun, leap into the dance!

As dark clouds roll, and towels take flight,
The socks just giggle with sheer delight.
For in the end, what's a little spin?
A story to tell where every sock can win!

The Sock Chronicles: A Comedic Saga

Once upon a couch, a sock did strut,
With a sassy seam and a tiny cut.
It gathered tales from every floor,
Of grand adventures and much more.

From laundry baskets where chaos reigns,
To wild escapades in the rain.
Each journey told with laughter and flair,
As the sock would boast of places rare.

"This one time, I sneaked out at night!
Joined a party of shoes, oh what a sight!
We danced on toes with a wild crew,
So many footsteps, I lost my view!"

Yet silence fell as darkness grew,
A lonely sock, just a bit askew.
But in its heart, the stories stayed,
A tapestry woven, with each escapade.

Fabricated Smiles in the Laundry

In the washroom, where bubbles rise,
Socks converse with playful sighs.
They trade secrets in quaint little chats,
About odd shirts and runaway hats.

"Oh, how I miss my perfect twin,
The matching pair who spun to win!"
A striped one adds, with a chuckle and grin,
"Maybe they've found a new life within!"

They stretch and fold, with fabrics that care,
Comedic tales in the steamy air.
Each spin a giggle, each rinse a jest,
In the realm of drying, they feel truly blessed.

And as the cycle comes to its end,
Bright colors shimmer, like a trusted friend.
Though some may go missing, others will stay,
In this fabric of humor, where socks find their way.

Frolicsome Footprints on the Floor

Little shoes with tiny tags,
Dance around the morning drags.
One is blue and one is red,
They tease each other, 'Time for bed!'

In corners, they begin to hide,
Playing games with utmost pride.
Behind the chair, a laugh does swell,
'Can you catch me? Only time will tell!'

A fun parade of fabric friends,
Together they'll make playful bends.
Chasing dust bunnies, what a sight,
Whirling 'round till fall of night.

Oh where have all the mates gone, though?
Just like whispers in the breeze that flow.
They vanish swift, like sneaky sprites,
Leaving lonely pairs in sights.

A Symphony of Wool and Whimsy

A melody of colors bright,
Socks perform a silly fight.
One's a polka, one's a stripe,
Twirling together in a hype.

They tumble, twist, and take a bow,
Shaking hands with kittens' meow.
A concert on the laundry floor,
Who knew wool could be such lore?

In cheerful checks and toe designs,
They dance like folk in rhythmic lines.
Spinning tales of joy and jest,
While their pairs are on a quest.

As giggles fill the vacant space,
They plot their next sock-footed race.
A tapestry of fun and cheer,
Woven snug, they persevere!

Serendipity in the Sock Drawer

In the drawers of softest cloth,
A curious chaos brews henceforth.
Tangled threads and colorful sights,
Search for pairs in merry fights.

A bright green wants to find its mate,
But it's all about the odds of fate.
Will it match the polka-dotted face?
Or stall for luck in this crazy space?

Old memories of evening runs,
Playful hops and winter suns.
These little scraps of fluff and thread,
Whisper stories long since said.

Amidst the mismatches and fuss,
Laughter rises, full of trust.
Each sock a part of tales of yore,
A wonderland forevermore!

Jests Among the Laundry Lines

There they hang in sunny rows,
Clothesline sagging, full of prose.
Breezes tease the playful white,
As they wave with pure delight.

An argyle and a floral friend,
Debate on who will bend and blend.
Riding gusts with cheerful flair,
Swaying proud in sunny air.

Faded patterns tell a tale,
Of muddy boots and puddles failed.
Each clip a memory draped with glee,
Lonely socks crave harmony.

As shadows stretch and daylight fades,
They tell of adventures, plans made.
With laughter sewn into each seam,
They weave the fabric of a dream.

The Frolics of Fabric Creatures

In a drawer where shadows play,
Cotton critters laugh all day.
Slipping, sliding, having fun,
In this game, chaos has begun.

One sock wears a silly hat,
While another dances like a cat.
With every twist, they take a spin,
Chasing threads, they cheer and grin.

They hold a feast of lint and fluff,
Beret and bowtie, oh so tough!
Around the room, they prance and glide,
In a joyful, unending slide.

But when we search, they're nowhere found,
In cozy corners, lost and bound.
Yet in their world, the fun won't cease,
For whimsical socks, bring endless peace.

The Curious Case of the Sock Bandit

Late at night, the heist begins,
Underneath the bed it spins.
A thief so sly, with sneaky paws,
Stealing warmth without a pause.

Whispers roam of vanished pairs,
Only one sock caught in snares.
Clotheslines tremble, tales unfold,
Of daring deeds, oh so bold!

With shadows leaping, sprightly glee,
The bandit wears a grand marquee.
Each foot's friend in a search so grand,
While sneaky giggles fill the land.

Yet in the day, they play it cool,
Back to laundry, oh what a fool.
Forever searching for what's lost,
In the tale of fun, they count the cost.

Whispers of Everyday Wonders

In the morning, light sneaks in,
Warmth and cheer, let the day begin.
Cupboards creak in gentle tunes,
As sunlight dances with the moon.

Moments sparkle, tiny sparks,
Underneath the park's old larks.
Drops of joy like rain fall down,
Spinning dreams in colorful town.

Curious ants play hide and seek,
Around the shoes and bricks they peek.
Laughter echoes, faint yet clear,
Every whisper draws us near.

Through the chaos, bright and fun,
Finding magic, never done.
In a world where giggles bloom,
Lost treasures hide in their own room.

The Dance of Lost Footwear

In the closet where umbrellas sway,
Footwear scrambles for a play day.
One boot hops, a sandal twirls,
As mismatched shoes whirl like pearls.

Chaos reigns as pairs take flight,
Dancing gaily through the night.
With every step, a laugh erupts,
In a flurry of fabric, they erupt.

The left turns right, a shoe parade,
As laughter rains in grand charade.
While slippers sneak behind the door,
A little giggle, "I want more!"

Oh, how they sway, on toes they prance,
In this wild, zany, funky dance.
For in the tangle of threads and cheer,
Each lost sole finds a partner near.

Uncharted Territory of Laundry

In the depths of the washer's embrace,
Colors collide, it's a wild race.
Someone's favorite sock, oh where did it go?
It vanished in froth, put on quite a show.

Tangled in mystery, fabric entwined,
Like a comedy sketch, it's truly unkind.
What once was a pair, now solo and free,
A twin on the run, just left for the spree.

Where do they wander, these footmates of fate?
Dancing through dryers, they must celebrate.
With each spin and tumble, they surely conspire,
To start a new trend, caught up in their fire.

We search high and low, in baskets and shelves,
Yet all we discover is dust from our elves.
So here's to the pairs that we might never see,
In the uncharted lands of lost laundry glee.

Threads of Joy Between Soles

Under the bed, there's a sock waiting there,
Peeking out shyly, with dust in its hair.
It's gathered some stories, of stairs it has climbed,
Grinning at secrets, now perfectly rhymed.

In the cupboard, they meet, mismatched and bold,
Leather and cotton, together unfold.
Spinning a tale of a whimsical night,
Where friends were made, under moon's merry light.

As the dryer spins on, the giggles commence,
A reunion of fabric, oh how it makes sense!
Twists and turns, it's a joyful ballet,
With every wash cycle, they dance and they play.

So sing for the socks that have traveled afar,
Across floors and fields, they've raised the bizarre.
It's not just attire, it's a journey of fun,
Underneath our feet, a celebration begun.

A Match Made in Drawers

In the realm of the drawers, a love story blooms,
Where polka dots meet stripes, in cozy costumes.
One shy argyle glances at bright neon hues,
Best friends forever, they've paid all their dues.

They chuckle and play, in the folds and the seams,
Whispering secrets, sharing their dreams.
A left foot and right foot, together they vibe,
Creating a duo that no one can bribe.

When the day draws near, they're both in a haze,
Waiting for hands to unveil them in glitz.
Once lost in the depths, now they're ready to shine,
A match made in fabrics, the stars align.

So gather your socks, for a grand jubilee,
Celebrate their unity, so wild and so free.
In every corner, those threads weave it right,
In the drawer of our hearts, they ignite pure delight.

The Sock Parade of Smiles

They march from the closet, a vibrant brigade,
Patterns and colors, together displayed.
From fuzzy to funky, they strut with delight,
A sock parade forms, what a marvelous sight!

They twirl and they whirl, in unison play,
Each stitch telling tales of their whimsical way.
With faces of joy, they shimmy on through,
Underfoot joy, in a jubilant view.

When a pair of old sneakers joins in the fun,
Socks leap to the rhythm, oh haven't they run?
Together they prance, in a dance of the bold,
In this kooky sock story, laughter unfolds.

And though every once in a while one may slip,
We'll cherish the journey, and give it a rip!
For in every lost sock, there's a tale that's been told,
A parade of bright memories, forever pure gold.

A Journey Through Knit and Purl

In a basket of yarn, colors collide,
Twists of fate where patterns abide.
Needles click in rhythm they play,
Creating a world where stitches array.

A scarf that becomes an unplanned quilt,
With holes and gaps like secrets built.
Each row a story, each stitch a cheer,
In this fabric realm, all joys appear.

Unexpected turn, oh what a twist!
A rogue loop awaits, unmissed.
With laughter echoing, we frolic and spin,
As woolen frays begin to grin.

Through knits and purls, we craft delight,
In every row, a playful sight.
With every twist, we giggle and play,
A whimsical journey, brightening our day.

Footloose and Fancy Free

In a dance of socks, mismatched and bold,
A happy parade of colors untold.
With one blue and one bright green hue,
They frolic around, a lively crew.

Two left feet, or maybe two right,
They spin and they twirl, a joyous sight.
Forgotten partners, lost in the race,
They prance on the floor, a comical chase.

Oh, where is the mate? A quest like no other,
For socks do not hide, but play with each other.
Under the couch or behind a chair,
Their playful antics fill the air.

Footloose they leap, with a wink and a grin,
Never taking heed of their mismatched kin.
In this cotton circus, they're wild and free,
A pair of comic relief, just let them be.

The Case of the Misplaced Heel

A sock detective with magnifying glass,
Searching high and low, oh what a farce!
Each clue leads to laughter, a trail of delight,
As socks play hide-and-seek, day and night.

A heel here, a toe there, such a riddle,
They dance like they're playing a merry fiddle.
In the depths of the drawer and behind each shoe,
Adventures unfold where socks grew and flew.

Whispers of yarn fill the air with glee,
As questions abound, where could they be?
A misfit crew with a playful aim,
Embracing their status in this silly game.

So here's to the socks with their whimsical plight,
A treasure hunt wrapped in pure delight.
For every lost heel finds a giggling friend,
In this comical journey, the fun never ends.

Warmth in Threads and Belly Laughs

In a cozy corner, laughter unfolds,
Where threads weave stories and warmth it holds.
A snuggly blanket, a giddy embrace,
With every stitch, we cherish this space.

A comedy of errors with needles in hand,
Creating a masterpiece, oh what a grand!
A loop that escapes, a yarn that unwinds,
In the warmth of our laughter, joy it finds.

Colorful patterns, a whimsical spree,
Woven together, endlessly free.
With each twist and turn, the giggles ignite,
As we cherish these threads, our hearts feel light.

So let us embrace this playful art,
With warmth in our souls and laughter to start.
In the tapestry of joy, we joyfully bask,
In the colorful threads of hilarity's task.

Twists and Turns of a Sockless Journey

In the dryer, they twirl and spin,
Yet one sails off, where should I begin?
Single and solo, all dressed up wrong,
Wandering feet hum a forgotten song.

Chasing the trail of a cotton refrain,
Through laundry rooms, it drives me insane.
One slips away, a sly little tease,
Who knew a sock could bring me to my knees?

Now mismatched pairs laugh in the breeze,
Each moment of searching brings giggles with ease.
With every step, my toes start to dance,
I'm on a quest, oh sweet sock romance!

So here I stand in a sock-less plight,
Exploring the world, my feet in delight.
Through twists and turns on this journey I roam,
Finding the rhythm of a missing sock home.

Whims of Woven Whimsy

In cozy corners, where oddities dwell,
Fabricated tales spin a yarn to tell.
A leap and a bounce, they mischievously hide,
These little dwellers in a cottony tide.

Legends unfold of the great sock escape,
In bright stripes and polka dots they drape.
With each little giggle, the mischief eludes,
Whimsical creatures in colorful moods.

They frolic and tumble in freshly washed glee,
Beneath the bed, where no one can see.
A riddle of threads, what a comical race,
Seeking companionship with a wrinkled embrace.

And as I snicker at their playful spree,
I find my own joy in this sock mystery.
For each missing piece brings a smile bright,
In the wacky world of woven delight.

Under the Couch: A Haunting Tale

Beneath the couch, the shadows grow deep,
A sock-boneyard where lost pairs creep.
Ghostly fabrics whisper secrets at night,
With mismatched cohorts, they take flight.

In a swirl of dust, they frolic with glee,
Eluding my grasp, they giggle with me.
Beneath the cushions, they dance and they prance,
This socky soiree, a silly romance.

Once lost to the void, now vivid with cheer,
They play hide-and-seek, so sly and sincere.
An eerie escape from the mundane pile,
Where odd little friends make the search worthwhile.

So I peek underneath for the fun they can share,
A laugh in the darkness, a friendship laid bare.
With each little venture where sock spirits roam,
I find joy anew in their ghostly home.

The Great Sock Search

In the early hours of a sunlit day,
I embark on a quest, come what may.
Through hampers aplenty and closets stretched wide,
I hunt for the mate that has jumped off the ride.

Behind the laundry basket, oh what a sight,
A mountain of fabric, chaos in flight.
Each twist and each turn brings new games to play,
Where's that rogue sock that ran away?

Fuzzy explorers, in a jungle of trends,
Beneath all the fabric, the laughter transcends.
With each little discovery of prints so bizarre,
I forget the lost moments and cheers from afar.

So let's celebrate all those mismatched delight,
For every solo sock, there's a story in sight.
Join the adventure in this fabric-filled jest,
In the great sock search, I'm truly blessed.

The Dance of Untethered Threads

Threaded journeys spin and sway,
A sock once bold has gone astray.
With twirls and flips, they take a chance,
In laundry's whirl, they find their dance.

Crisp and clean, they wave hello,
But where's the other? Who could know?
Colors bright in staggering pairs,
A sock parade with empty chairs.

Whispers tease in every fold,
Of stories woven, yet untold.
A solo act on wooden floor,
A faded pattern seeks the door.

So let them twirl, these wayward strips,
In a world of mismatches, joy equips.
As laughter echoes through the room,
Untethered threads, like sprites, they bloom.

Where Did My Cozy Companion Go?

In a pile of fluff, I thought it clear,
One squishy friend that I held dear.
But check, and check, he's slipped away,
Now chilly toes decide to play.

The feline snickers as I pout,
He knows the secret, there's no doubt.
Tickled pink by my distressed face,
He prowls around in playful grace.

Washed in laughter, dreams in bright hues,
Yet I find myself with only one shoe.
The couch is a place of socky lore,
Where tangled threads whisper 'more, more!'

Oh cozy pal, a thief at bay,
Steal my warmth, and dance away.
With every wash, the mystery grew,
A sock's adventure, but who knew?

In Search of Stray Footwear

Beneath the bed, what do I see?
A rogue slip-on, wild and free.
With bouncy steps, he doesn't hide,
In sock hide-and-seek, he'll take pride.

Chasing shadows, I must act fast,
For time with footwear never lasts.
In corners dark, and crannies deep,
A missing mate? A secret keep.

The dryer sings a lonesome tune,
In the cycle's spin, they croon and swoon.
Oh how they twirl in misty air,
Lost companions, twinkling flair.

Yet still I smile in mismatched fun,
Each runaway brings a little pun.
In oddity, there's joy, it's true,
Two solo socks share a giggle, too.

The Secrets of the Matching Drawer

In the drawer, a realm so neat,
Pairs aligned in a warm retreat.
Yet somehow, one slips from the pack,
Only to find it must come back.

The whispers of cotton and thread,
Sing secrets where lone socks are led.
Adventures through wash cycles unfold,
With tales of mischief, bright and bold.

Each fabric smooth, some worn with grace,
Yet all have stories in their place.
Reunions spark with joyous cheers,
Of friends once lost, now free of fears.

So rummage through that tangled space,
Find joy in each wiggly trace.
For in the mismatched, laughter swells,
In every sock, a tale compels.

Embracing the Unmatched and the Silly

In pairs they start, a bold array,
One vanishes, to play a game of sway.
Left behind, its partner looks forlorn,
A dance of solitude since the day was born.

Colors clash in wild disarray,
Bold stripes and dots in contrast, they stay.
Together they laugh, each foolish band,
Finding joy in mismatched, a quirky stand.

Each step forward, a quirky trail,
Laughter echoes, as soles set sail.
Unruly antics of those lone socks,
Bring cheer to the dance floor of mismatched rocks.

Celebrate the jest, the quirky cheer,
In every fabric, a story near.
Frolic with joy, let madness flow,
In pairs or alone, we relish the show.

Twirling Through Time with Wobbly Footwear

With every spin, they join the fun,
Echoes of giggles spark the run.
One shoe bounces, the other lags,
Joyfully hopping like two silly hags.

Footwear floating, no steps in line,
Each twist and turn, the stars align.
Wobbly antics, a dizzying race,
In silly shoes, we find our place.

A trip, a slide, the giggles soar,
As soles stumble through the open door.
Unstable journey, yet hearts are light,
In chaos we dance, from day to night.

Celebrate each tumble, each grind and scratch,
In joyous missteps, there's nothing to catch.
Embrace each moment, the wild parade,
For in every wobble, new memories are made.

Unexpected Delights in Everyday Threads

A gentle tug, a pull and tease,
Such moments sparkle, a breeze to please.
Hidden treasures 'neath fabric's embrace,
In frayed seams laughter finds its space.

Colors collide, a joyful scheme,
Threads entwined in a wild dream.
Each hem a story, a twist of fate,
Unexpected giggles, we celebrate.

Socks upside down, oh what a sight,
A comedy play, with fabric's delight.
As patterns meet in a tangled sway,
The threads unravel, pushing gloom away.

In the cupboard's corner, surprises grow,
Every errant thread has a tale to show.
Embracing the quirks in each tiny seam,
Adventure awaits, where silliness beams.

A Chuckle in Every Corner of the Closet

Behind the door, those treasures sigh,
Each fabric whispers of days gone by.
A lone button dances, a twinkle in sight,
As shadows chuckle in morning light.

Amidst the dust, a forgotten shoe,
Echoes the laughter of the lively crew.
Be it frayed, be it torn, it holds a spark,
Of memories made where we once embarked.

In cluttered corners, joy takes flight,
As mismatched threads weave through the night.
Each piece a puzzle, a riddle wrapped,
In the heart of the closet, tales are tapped.

So swing wide the doors, let the stories spill,
In the chaotic charm, we embrace the thrill.
For every garment has a chuckle to share,
In the symphony of fabric, there's magic in the air.

A Humorist's Guide to Stranded Socks

In the dryer, a sock takes flight,
Spinning tales in the endless night.
Pair of polka dots, oh what a sight,
With a lonely stripe, out of sheer delight.

Mismatched friends in a basket roam,
One like a wanderer, far from home.
Lurking in corners, they start to moan,
Yearning for warmth, but destined to groan.

A sock puppet show, we all can see,
Glorious stories, wrapped in glee.
With laughter echoing, what could it be?
Celebrating socks, just you and me.

So heed the tale of the wandering pair,
Embrace the chaos, beyond despair.
For joy in the missing is truly rare,
In a world full of socks, show you care.

The Enchanted Sock Kingdom

In a realm where soft threads meet,
Lurking socks dance on nimble feet.
Woolen wizards cast spells so sweet,
Creating games that none could defeat.

The king, a funky, fuzzy shoe,
Rules a court of colors, bright and true.
With mismatched subjects in every hue,
Happiness blooms in the whimsical view.

Fairy floss lands on a cotton cloud,
Where socks twirl around, laughing loud.
In a tapestry woven, they feel proud,
As giggles form a joyful crowd.

So come, dear wanderer, take a peek,
Visit the kingdom and hear them speak.
In every fiber, fun's at its peak,
In a world of socks, forever unique.

Unraveling Laughter in Cotton

Threads that tangle with endless cheer,
A chase through the laundry, nothing to fear.
With each lost partner, we share a tear,
Yet their adventures are always near.

Sneaky socks go on secret quests,
Finding lost keys, sparking playful jests.
On a magic carpet that never rests,
Their charming capers outshine all tests.

A sing-along echoes through the air,
As once-shy socks toss away despair.
In whirling bliss, they happily share,
Joy in their travels, without a care.

So laugh with socks on their daring spree,
In each little fold, their glee is free.
Celebrate the quirky, come and see,
How missing friends can still be with thee.

Solitary Footwear and the Purse of Joy

A lone sock sits with a wistful grin,
Dreaming of days with buddies akin.
With missing mates, how can they win?
But hope springs forth in the softest skin.

In a world of pockets, hidden away,
A solitary shoe finds a place to stay.
Conversations with dust bunnies sway,
Creating a tale for a sunny day.

The purse of joy carries whispers bright,
Of vanished fellows lost from sight.
Yet each little fabric, stitched with delight,
Holds moments of laughter, shining light.

So treasure the lost, the bold and the shy,
In every sock's journey, a reason to fly.
For in the oddness, we learn to rely,
On the humor of life that never says bye.

The Curious Case of the Wayward Heels

In a drawer they loved to hide,
Beneath pajama bottoms, side by side.
They squabbled on fashion, all on display,
Yet one went missing, slipped away.

They gossip in whispers, oh what a scene,
Do others feel left out, or are they just mean?
A tango of fabric, a frolic of thread,
The stories they weave, the fun that they spread.

Under beds where dust bunnies play,
A heel, once proud, now gone astray.
Upside-down worlds of twisted twine,
Revealing a riddle, oh so fine!

In a basket of laundry, they make their stand,
Announcing their quirks with a colorful band.
But once the spin cycle wraps them tight,
Who knows what's hiding from our sight?

Socks in Disguise: A Comedic Journey

In the land of laundry, bold and bright,
A pair conspired to take flight.
They donned masks made from scraps of lace,
Chasing dreams in a daring race.

With a wink and a twist, they'd twist and twirl,
Pretending to be a fashionable girl.
They'd giggle at sneakers, oh, what a show!
While spinning on toes - where did they go?

In puddles of socks, secrets unfurled,
Clashing patterns caused quite a whirl.
A sock in a cap, a sock in a cape,
Transforming their styles, no need for escape!

But one sock vanished, the tale goes on,
Remnants of fabric, the spirit still strong.
In this grand adventure, laughter ignites,
As socks-on-the-run conquer silly heights!

Whimsical Twists on the Clothesline

Hoisted up high where the breezes hum,
Fabric friends gather, oh, what a drum!
A blue polka-dot sharing tales of the night,
While stripes dance cheeky in the soft twilight.

In bright summer sun, they sway and prance,
Entwined in the clothesline, they perfect their dance.
Whirls of color creating a show,
When a rogue wind appears, watch how they go!

But amidst the sway, a mystery brews,
Lost in the folds, who will choose?
A stray sock chuckles from a secretive nook,
Holding a treasure, let's take a look.

Questions remain in the tangled seams,
Is it a sock or a cloak of dreams?
Within each twist and every flaring sound,
Laughter persists where lost things are found!

Where Secrets Hide in Soft Fibers

In drawers tucked tight, treasures await,
Soft pairs with stories link up their fate.
They whisper of antics, of silly things keen,
The secrets they keep, oh, how they gleam.

A cozy confessional, each fold has a say,
Revealing the antics of a typical day.
Once they were loyal, matching their flair,
Now playful pretenders burlap and air!

Rolled in the corners, a rogue sock plots,
Dreaming of capers within all the knots.
A lawless venture in the fabric realm,
Each twist a joke at the humor helm.

So while one goes missing and laughter swells,
A sock-saga unfolds and twinkle it tells.
In the warm embrace where fibers intertwine,
The joy of the chase—a perfect design!

Happiness in Worn-Out Soles

In the corner, pairs do roam,
With holes that tell a tale of home.
Each step a giggle, a cheerfully dance,
Flip-flops and slippers join in the prance.

Sandals sway in summer's glow,
Chasing shadows, putting on a show.
With every tread, a story unfolds,
Of adventures where laughter boldly molds.

A shoe without a match, oh dear!
Maybe it's off saving another's cheer.
Yet through this jumbled, joyful mess,
A melody of fun, which we confess.

Oh, happiness lives in worn-out threads,
In every stich where laughter spreads.
Feet are dancing to whimsy's song,
In forgotten soles where we all belong.

Socks on a Windy Day

Bright stripes swirl in a playful gale,
Whimsical patterns begin to sail.
A footloose dance on a breezy lane,
Cotton clouds lifting joy's refrain.

Pulled from the drawer like a magic trick,
Fancy pairs, do they match? Time will pick.
Catching the wind as they leap and twirl,
Frolicsome fun, a fabric whirl.

With every gust, a slice of delight,
Fluffy buddies take off in flight.
Laughter echoes as they float away,
Socks, oh socks, put on a display!

When the breezes stop and stillness falls,
Will they find their way back to the walls?
Perhaps in the sun where colors play,
Magic awaits on a windy day.

Echoes of Unseen Giggles

In a closet where secrets sleep,
Beneath the chaos, whispers creep.
Echoes of chuckles, faint yet bright,
Muffled mirth in the soft twilight.

Pairs that wander, one left behind,
Chasing the others, to be aligned.
Tickled threads in a fabric spree,
A hidden riot of glee and spree.

Stitched with stories of playful days,
In every fold, a mystery stays.
Fuzzy friends who took a leap,
Finding joy in the laughter they keep.

So when you search, take a pause to hear,
The hushing giggles that draw ever near.
In shadows of drawers, joy will bloom,
As unseen laughter fills the room.

The Sock Monologue

Ladies and gents, I present to you,
A tale of my kind, sometimes askew.
Stitched in humor, we play our part,
In laundry's limelight, we steal the heart.

Oh, the drama when a dryer roars,
Pairs get lost behind tumbling doors.
One goes out, the other stays home,
In a sock-ly world where we roam.

Are we mismatched or just unique?
A jazz of colors, a life so chic!
From polka dots to stripes we prance,
Giving warmth as we twist and dance.

So here's to the souls in cotton guise,
Each missed companion, a joyful surprise.
With every disappearance, a chance to jest,
In the sock saga, we're truly blessed.

Unraveled Threads of Humor

In a land where odd pairs roam,
Lone socks dance, far from home.
With stripes and dots, they twirl and spin,
Fleeing the mundane, let the fun begin.

A sock brigade in a drawer's embrace,
Chasing fluff on a never-ending race.
Giggles echo in the laundry night,
As mismatched pairs take to flight.

From the depths of the washing drum,
Comes a riddle, a sock-shaped hum.
Who knew that warmth could lead astray,
To grand adventures in disarray?

As tales unfold in a fabric arc,
Every thread holds a cheerful spark.
In worlds where socks have space to play,
We find the joy that socks convey.

Footprints of Frayed Memories

A twist in time, a sock found near,
Whispers of laughter, a heart cheers.
In the echoes of fabric fate,
Every encounter seals the date.

Once belonged to someone shy,
Now a champion, soaring high.
With every step, a tale to tell,
Of the mischief where lost socks dwell.

When the wind blows through the week,
A pair of socks may start to sneak.
Tripping over moments past,
Saving smiles, hoping they last.

With frayed edges and memories bright,
They dance along, a comical sight.
Each thread pulls stories from afar,
Unraveling joy, like a shooting star.

When the Dryer Dances

With a whirl and a twirl, they begin to sway,
Spinning around in a snug ballet.
A sock parade in the tumbler's spin,
Grooving together with a soft, warm grin.

A tumble here, a toss over there,
Fluffy delights in the swirling air.
In the heat of the night, tales set free,
As pairs go missing, oh where could they be?

Every cycle brings giggles anew,
As bright colors clash with a hue askew.
In the land of lint, they share a song,
With shrieks of joy that echo along.

Round and round, the clothes collide,
Bringing laughter on the inside.
When the machine's hum becomes a tune,
We join in as socks vanish too soon.

The Sock That Vanished in Time

Once upon a floor, in patterned glee,
A sock set off on an odyssey.
Into the realm of forgotten space,
A feisty little footsie with an adventurous pace.

Through the sofa's fluff and under the bed,
It traveled in search of a market thread.
Like a hero in silence, it yearned to roam,
Adventuring realms far from its home.

With a twist of fate, it found a way,
Into laundry lore, where mismatched play.
Each corner of the house held suspense,
As it danced with dust mites, a whirlwind experience.

In the great unknown, friendships formed tight,
Unexpected allies in fabric flight.
Though it vanished from view, never fear,
In laughter and memories, it lingers near.

Threads of Happiness Unraveled

A tumble here and a spin to there,
Bright colors dance without a care.
A single shoe finds its left-side mate,
While lonely socks mourn their own fate.

In corners dark, they plot and scheme,
To weave a tale of a vanished dream.
They dodge the wash and evade the fold,
Trading stories of warmth untold.

The dryer hums a secret tune,
As mismatched pairs embrace the moon.
With giggles soft, they swirl and spin,
In every fold, a cheeky grin.

Through all the spins and all the shakes,
They twirl with joy, no time for aches.
For in this mess, a fun surprise,
Life's silly dance, oh how it flies.

Sunlit Moments and Forgotten Pairs

In sunlight bright, socks fall like rain,
One's striped, one's polka; a merry chain.
They stretch their limbs, they bask and play,
While the dryer dreams of a sunny day.

A sock with spots finds a floral friend,
Together they giggle, the fun won't end.
Tales of mishaps, of trips and slips,
Adventures long, in secret scripts.

They peek from baskets, their heads held high,
Winking and nodding, oh my, oh my!
For every pair that's lost at sea,
A single soul claims wild jubilee.

The dance of fabric, the sway of fun,
In every laugh, a story spun.
While one may wander, don't feel too blue,
In every tangle, there's joy anew.

Giggling in the Laundry Basket

A heap of fluff in a woven nest,
Beneath the warmth, they giggle and jest.
Bright hues collide, a vibrant show,
In the laundry basket, the fun will grow.

Unruly socks, they play their tricks,
Hiding behind sheets, such clever picks.
With whispers soft, they plot to roam,
To visit the kitchen, to claim the home.

Chasing buttons, wrapping up tight,
In every corner, pure delight.
Faded patterns dance on the floor,
While mismatched pairs shout, "We want more!"

They tumble and stretch in a twisty glee,
Each twist and turn, a jubilee.
For in this chaos, they feel alive,
A funny crew that loves to thrive.

The Mysterious Disappearance of Sockmates

In a world where pairs have been unmade,
Solo socks wander, unafraid.
They creep and crawl on a quest remote,
With tales of missing, they happily gloat.

"Where did you go?" a blue one cries,
With a wink and a nod, the striped one replies.
"We danced with the dust bunnies, oh what a thrill,
Listen closely now, it's a wild, wild spill!"

Socks in the shadows, on a secret quest,
Every tumble dryer hides a jest.
While some may vanish without a trace,
Others giggle through that fluffy space.

In mismatched moments, they learn to blend,
To find the joy that never has to end.
For though they're parted, their spirits soar,
In the realm of fabric, they laugh evermore.

Warped Patterns of Happiness

In the drawer, a funny sight,
Colors clash, a pure delight.
Stripes and spots, they dance around,
A quirky warmth in chaos found.

Each piece a tale, a jumbled cheer,
Whispers of joy in fabric near.
A sock brigade, they march in line,
Hand in hand, they twist and twine.

The dryer sings a clever tune,
While mismatched pairs start to swoon.
Joyful steps, a clumsy thread,
A journey shared, where none dare tread.

Fabric laughs in silly schemes,
Binding hearts with playful dreams.
In folds and wrinkles, smiles unfold,
A garment's hug, a warmth retold.

Threads of Whimsy Underfoot

On the floor, a rogue sock peeks,
A hero's tale in cotton speaks.
Jumps and twirls, a merry chase,
In secret corners, finds its place.

Pairs may hide and run away,
But still they dance, come what may.
Stray threads spin a happy whirl,
In every nook, a sock's twirl.

Socks unite in laughter's grip,
Creating pathways for a trip.
Beneath the couch, a mystery,
Two hearts entwined, just meant to be.

With every step, a giggle springs,
A silent tune their movement sings.
In every tumble, joy they wring,
A playful dance, oh what a fling!

The Sock That Roamed the World

Once a sock with dreams so grand,
Set off to roam an unknown land.
Through puddles deep and grassy fields,
Adventures burst, the freedom yields.

In cafes bright, it sipped some tea,
Spun stories wild, so carefree.
Talked to shoes, and hats, and more,
A wanderer, it loved to soar.

From mountain peaks to valleys low,
It danced with snowflakes, stole the show.
In every step, a punchline brewed,
A world of laughs, a joyous mood.

At night it dreamed of cozy beds,
Tales of mischief wrapped in threads.
Homeward bound, it twirled and swirled,
The legend of the sock that twirled.

Clashes in the Laundry Universe

In the basket, a socky war,
Colors battle, call for more.
Whites taunt darks, and reds join in,
A riot starts, a bold sock spin.

Cuffs collide and stripes declare,
Patterns weaving through the air.
"Join our team!" the polka dots shout,
While old jeans reminisce about.

The whirlpool spins, a washing fight,
All in good fun, nothing's slight.
When the rinse sets them free,
They share a laugh, just wait and see.

Emerging fresh, they find a way,
To pair up in a wacky play.
In this universe, smiles ignite,
Socks united, oh what a sight!

Lost and Found: A Textile Odyssey

In drawers where fabrics intertwine,
A footless wanderer starts to whine.
Where's the mate that danced in pairs?
This laundry saga's full of snares.

A tumble dryer spins the tale,
Of linty trails and socks that sail.
From soft depths of forgotten sheets,
Emerges a quest for warm, snug feats.

Behind the couch, a sock does peek,
With a cheeky grin, it starts to speak.
'I've traveled far, please don't despair!'
Together now, they laugh and share.

In glory found, they twirl and sway,
No more alone, they dance and play.
An adventure spun in hues so bright,
The little knights of cozy night.

The Sock That Found Its Way Home

Once lost in a world of black and white,
A lone sock yearned for the warmth of night.
It rolled through streets, through puddles and mud,
Seeking its pair with a sense of flood.

It dodged a cat and a sneaky shoe,
Its heart was light; it just wanted you.
Through tangled hedges and garden gnomes,
A silly quest to return to its home.

At last it neared the prideful door,
One last leap onto the hardwood floor.
With joy, it spotted its long-lost mate,
Together again, two souls celebrate.

Now snug in a drawer, a tale of glee,
Adventure so grand, just wait and see!
No longer apart, together they rest,
In a cozy embrace, oh, socks are the best!

Giggles Among the Garments

In the realm where tidying's a must,
Giggles arise from heaps of dust.
A shirt chuckles, a tie starts to dance,
As mismatched pairs give socks a chance.

Pajamas prance on a sunbeam bright,
While old shorts grumble about the night.
A skirt sways with a twinkling shout,
'Join the fun! Let's twist about!'

Button eyes gleam from plushy spree,
They plot a parade of quirky glee.
Among the garments, joy takes its reign,
In a fashion show that defies the mundane.

Each soft fabric shares a story untold,
Of fades, escapes, and colors bold.
In a fabric fiesta, let laughter combine,
For among these garments, the spirits align.

Patchwork Memories of Forgotten Footwear

Once a pair that danced with glee,
A patchwork dream of harmony.
Now scattered stories in forgotten seams,
Whispers of warmth in cotton dreams.

From corners thick with dust of years,
A sing-along of cozy cheers.
Through seasons turned and patterns aged,
They recount the tales that life has staged.

One sock recalls a rainy day,
Sliding in puddles, oh what a play!
The other smiles at the tales they spun,
Of adventures shared and endless fun.

Though distances stretch and colors fade,
In patchwork memories, joys never stayed.
Forever stitched with laughter's thread,
In the heart where all socks are wed.

The Errant Sock's Journey

One sock goes missing, it's quite a game,
With a twist and a wiggle, we're not quite the same.
It danced through the air, from the wash it did flee,
Now the lonely one waits, just as sad as can be.

It hid in the closet, with shoes in a pile,
Whispering secrets with an old, dusty smile.
While socks on their own, in the breeze had a blast,
This one's stuck dreaming of the fun it had past.

A match made in chaos, a pair gone astray,
Why do they wander, I'm left here to say?
As pairs come together, this one falls aside,
On a quest for adventure, new paths it must bide.

With colors so bright, it still spins and twirls,
Across fields of lint, through the fabric it whirls.
Though it longs for its buddy, it won't cry in vain,
For happiness dances amidst all the pain.

The Colorful Odyssey of Footwear

In the land of the laundry, socks take their stand,
A riot of colors, all perfectly planned.
Yet one took a leap, and flew off with the breeze,
Leaving its partner in a soft, cotton squeeze.

Pair by pair, they once had a ball,
But one picked a route that led straight to the wall.
Now mismatched and lonesome, it lounges around,
Dreaming of adventures where fun should abound.

Oh, the sights that it's seen! The things that it's done,
From the depths of the dryer to bright rays of sun.
Yet still does it ponder, with a soft little sigh,
How it danced in the day while its twin stayed nearby.

So here's to the wanderers, off track for a while,
May they find joyful journeys, and slip into style.
Though one is a wanderer, together they'll weave,
A tale of bright threads that we all can believe.

Chronicles from the Depths of the Drawer

Deep in the drawer, a sock takes a nap,
With a million old stories, and crumbs in its lap.
Each fold tells of laughter, each wrinkle a cheer,
From mismatched adventures, it holds so dear.

A rogue from the wash makes a case for the brave,
While lounging with buttons, it dreams of the wave.
Oh, the gentle tumble of nights spent so bold,
With shirts that spun tales, and secrets untold.

Adventure awakes in the shadows it keeps,
Of gatherings missed, yet still in a heap.
For every lone wanderer, a partner awaits,
On the path through the drawer, where destiny fates.

So raise up a cheer for the sock in repose,
With threads intertwined, let the friendship compose.
Through crumples and chaos, together they laugh,
An odyssey lived in this comfortable path.

Stitches in Time: A Comedic Reflection

Oh, what fate has befallen these pairs on the line?
One's off to the circus, while the other's just fine.
They go on adventures, one wild and free,
While the other just searches for where it should be.

From mismatched escapades to socks lost in crowds,
They giggle and tumble, under living room shrouds.
One sings of the disco, while the other just snores,
As they trade their wild tales, behind closet doors.

With the flipping of fortunes, this life is a tease,
Where one struts in style, and the other's a breeze.
Yet each thread is a treasure, a wink and a smile,
Celebrating their journey, they'll hang out a while.

So cherish the moments, let mismatched be bold,
For laughter and chaos, these stories unfold.
In a world of the quirky, we stand side by side,
A bond made of fabric, forever our pride.

Unruly Pairs and Chuckles Aloud

In every drawer, a playful mess,
Stray companions in a tangled dress.
One's a polka dot, the other a stripe,
They dance on the floor, oh what a type!

Laughter erupts with every slip,
As mismatched buddies start to flip.
A pair that's meant for shoes no more,
Join in a jig on the kitchen floor!

Oh, the antics of a runaway sock,
Sampling adventures, with a tick-tock clock.
Each twist and turn proves quite absurd,
As socks play tag, they're rarely deterred!

With every tumble, the humor grows,
A cabinet of chaos, as everyone knows.
Unruly pairs that bring joy so bright,
In their hapless dance, they feel just right!

The Quest for the Wayward Sock

In the depths of the dryer, a treasure awaits,
One lone sock whispers, escaping the fates.
Adventurous heart, it ventures alone,
While its mate waits, forlorn and unknown.

On the laundry line, a hero's plight,
Who knew such fabric could cause such a fright?
Through mud and through rain, a journey galore,
Seeking the fabric soul, forevermore!

A sock on a mission, so gallant and free,
Escaping the wringer, oh let it be!
With every spin, each tumble and whirl,
The quest intertwines with a brave little twirl.

Yet back in the home, the other does sigh,
Missing its mate, a longing up high.
With laughter we ponder, where can it be?
This quest for the sock is quite the mystery!

Joyful Steps and Silly Socks

Tiptoe, stumble, giggle and hop,
Socks strive to dance, never want to stop.
With every twist, they whirl around,
Their colorful prints, the best to be found!

Oh, the fun in a mismatched pair,
Stripes with spots, an eccentric flair.
They trot through puddles, through grass so green,
In a world of whimsy, where none can be mean.

Slides and glides, a merriment spree,
Socks in a chorus, singing with glee!
Silly adventures, laughter explodes,
As they conquer the steps and the winding roads.

Every stubbed toe tells a tale so bright,
Of socks that defy the limiting sight.
Joyful steps, with every carefree kick,
In the garden of mirth, our antics run thick!

Where Humor Meets Missing Threads

A sock with a hole, it chuckles with glee,
While one says, 'Please, don't abandon me!'
In corners they fester, mismatched and free,
Together they weave a tapestry.

In the land of washed cotton, a kingdom in sight,
They skedaddle around in merry delight.
Where do ones wander when pairs are askew?
As a sock gallivants, it finds a new view.

Threads tugging gently, telling their tales,
Of socks on adventures, through sun and through gales.
With some silly mishaps, oh what a tease,
This court of the lost is bound to please!

So here's to the cheeky, the brave, and the bold,
In the sock world of humor, stories unfold.
Laughter erupts as the truth comes to light,
In a wardrobe of whimsy, they shine ever bright!

Soleful Journeys and Unexpected Giggles

In a drawer where they all reside,
A pair of mismatched dreams collide.
One's got stripes, the other's a plaid,
Together they dance, oh life isn't bad.

With each step, they stumble and twirl,
Bringing smiles to every boy and girl.
They jump and jive, a silly sight,
Making mischief, spreading delight.

When laundry day comes, they play hide and seek,
In tunnels of fabric, they sneak and peek.
While the washer spins, they plot and scheme,
A world of wonder, a sock puppet dream.

Out of the wash, they emerge anew,
With stories and giggles, adventures in view.
These tiny foot soldiers, brave and so bold,
In their cozy kingdom, their tales unfold.

The Adventures of the One-Eyed Sock

Once a sock lost its partner, it's true,
With one lonely eye, it had much to do.
It rolled down the hall, a brave little rogue,
Seeking out stories wherever it trod.

A pair of shoes laughed, "What a sight to see,
A sock on a quest, oh so carefree!"
Through puddles and puddings, it hopped with glee,
Waving goodbye to the life once so free.

Its journey was wild, but it missed its mate,
A twinge of longing, now that was fate.
Yet with each twist and turn on the floor,
The one-eyed sock found joy in the roar.

And when it returned, with tales to tell,
A sock full of charm, its stories do swell.
No need for a pair, just laughter around,
In the land of the lost, true friendship is found.

Fables of Fabric and Folly

In the realm of laundry, madness ensues,
Bright patterns dance, all the colors amuse.
A fabric's tale, with mischief at heart,
Where each twirl spins laughter, a true work of art.

Fluffy white clouds join a dapper red crew,
They tango on counters, what a funny view.
The dryer's a stage, where the bold take a chance,
In a whirl of fluff, they all join in the dance.

One sock with polka dots shares a giggle,
While a missing mate sits quiet, then wiggles.
"Oh where did you wander?" it asks with a sigh,
But the other just grins, "Oh, I learned how to fly!"

Through tumble and twist, they find joy galore,
Each fabric tells tales, who could ask for more?
For every lost match, there's a story to weave,
In the soft world of textiles, it's magic we believe.

Hidden Treasures of Cozy Confusion

In corners of closets, secrets reside,
Hidden treasures where odd socks have lied.
A basket of wonders, mismatched and bold,
Each one with a story patiently told.

"Oh dear!" says a striped one, lost in the fray,
"What happened to my friend on this crazy day?"
The checkered one chuckles, "Let's make it a game,
We'll find you a buddy, and no one's to blame."

From under the bed to the back of the shoe,
They venture together, this brave little crew.
A polka-dot sock spins, and a plaid one does cheer,
Creating a circus with laughter, oh dear!

So gather your socks, don't let them feel blue,
For each one is special, they giggle just for you.
In their cozy confusion, joy fills the air,
For every lost pair, there's a treasure to share.

www.ingramcontent.com/pod-product-compliance
Lightning Source LLC
Chambersburg PA
CBHW051643160426
43209CB00004B/777